Lean Recruitment:

Finding Better Talent Faster

• • •

Lean Recruitment:

Finding Better Talent Faster

Gary Romano and Alison LaRocca

ISBN: 1974253864
ISBN 13: 9781974253869
Library of Congress Control Number: 2017912169
CreateSpace Independent Publishing Platform
North Charleston, South Carolina

Civitas Strategies, LLC, Lynnfield, MA (www.civstrat.com)

Table of Contents

Author's Acknowledgements

First and foremost, the authors would like to thank their colleagues Bonnie Clapp and Abby King, who were both kind enough to lend their wisdom and experience to the project and were instrumental in developing both the manuscript and the Lean Recruitment approach.

The authors would also like to thank Jillian Hasner, a true friend and colleague. Without her encouragement and support, there would be no Lean Recruitment or Access HR. As CEO of Take Stock in Children, one of the nation's premier college readiness organizations (www.takestockinchildren.org), Jillian was an early adopter of Lean Recruitment and continues to be one of its strongest champions.

Gary Romano would like to personally thank Alison LaRocca, his "partner in crime" at Civitas Strategies and Access HR. Alison's vision and insights were critical to shaping the development of this book and, more importantly, the Lean Recruitment approach. Gary would also like to thank his wife, Karen O'Brien, and The

Romano Boys, Ben and Finn, for putting up with the development of a second book in as many years. This work coming to fruition is a direct result of their patience and sacrifice.

Alison LaRocca would personally like to thank her family for their unwavering support of her endeavors. She is forever grateful.

Introduction by Gary Romano

I will always remember the first person I had to fire.

I was a young manager, fresh out of graduate school, and working for a consultancy. I had been given the opportunity to hire my first staff member, to meet burgeoning demands in our research unit. I had hired people before, as a manager in a retail bookstore chain, and thought hiring for this position would be a similar experience.

I did everything "by the book." I put an advertisement on some of the local sites, emailed it to some friends, and waited for the candidates to roll in. To my surprise, the flood of applicants I had expected ended up being a trickle, most of whom were completely unqualified. Within the slim pool, I did find one person; a clear risk, but the best in the bunch. I made the pitch to the owner of the firm and the candidate was hired that day.

Much to my chagrin, I quickly found out my hire was not up to the task. This person wasn't motivated by the work, couldn't pursue tasks independently, and had a habit of showing up late and leaving early; that is, when they bothered to show up at all. I did everything I could to get them on-track: mentoring, serious conversations, even completing some of the person's work myself, in hopes that I could guilt them into a putting forth a better effort. In the end, I admitted defeat and let the person go. I wasn't happy when they left, feeling completely disheartened for the person and for myself.

My experience 20 years ago isn't that different from what many leaders and business owners experience regularly; a poor hire can be the greatest determent to any organization. As a reader of this book, you may very well have experienced the same. Yet you probably also know, from personal experience, that hiring quality candidates on the first try is not a simple process.

How many of these scenarios sound familiar?

* You advertise a job in every possible outlet you can think about, yet receive few applicants in return for your efforts. The ones you do get are barely qualified for the position. You know the job is an attractive one for people in your field, but somehow, you just are not able to connect with the talent you need.
* Over 100 people apply for a position, but as you review resumes you realize that many of them misunderstood

the qualifications for the job. Most are far too inexperienced or underqualified for the position. What once seemed to be a large pool of candidates has now been reduced to a handful.

* Your search team sits down to review a pool of talented people, only to realize that the ideal candidate needs to possess one specific subset of the skills you advertised for. When you consider those with the identified skill-set, your list of potential interviewees has now been reduced to a handful of candidates- none of whom were at the top of your list. You are forced to choose between interviewing candidates within the subset, and those who are highly-qualified, but don't meet the exact skill requirements.

As if the recruiting process wasn't already challenging enough, you also know there is now more competition for talent than ever. Also, the talent you hire needs to have a broader skillset than ever before. You need candidates with expertise in both the subject matter directly related to the position, and the ever-changing array of technologies found in the workplace. You need employees who are more independent, more innovative, and more entrepreneurial, to stay competitive in your chosen market.

This is even more acute if you are in a location that is less accessible to top talent, like rural areas with smaller populations or conversely, urban areas where strong candidates can command higher salaries.

These challenges may lead you to seek help in finding the best talent possible. At the most basic level, there are three pathways you can take:

1. Hiring a Human Resources Staff – This is a great option if possible. However, most small- and medium-sized nonprofits and businesses cannot afford an HR staff. If you do have one, they may be consumed with onboarding new hires, managing benefits, and maintaining paperwork. Your HR staff member might play multiple roles within the organization, which doesn't leave much time or energy to devote to finding the highest quality talent.
2. Financial Incentives – This option includes offering signing bonuses or an increased salary and benefits to preferred candidates. This can be an effective option; however, if you are a tight-profit margin operation, this could be similarly impossible to even consider from a financial standpoint.
3. Engaging the Services of a Recruiting Firm – This is often the most effective means for tapping into an extensive network of talent. This can be a good option; however, the costs of the project and the time it takes to implement may mean that this pathway is out of reach for most smaller organizations. For others, is only an option for recruiting the top positions, such as a CEO or Executive Director.

It was these imperfect choices that led my firm, Civitas Strategies (http://www.civstrat.com), to develop a new method for smaller organizations to find the talent they so desperately need. I call this process Lean Recruiting.

Lean Recruiting is:

* Effective – Our clients report that the talent found via this method is on par with, if not better than, candidates they have found using traditional recruiting strategies or firms.
* Cost-effective – Lean Recruiting allows our clients to find talent for half the cost of professional recruiting firms, and can be self-executed with existing staff.
* Timely – Organizations can go from the decision to hire to making a job offer to a preferred candidate, on average, 40% faster than with traditional recruiting methods.

A Long Strange Trip

Civitas Strategies is a consultancy focused on helping nonprofits to grow their impact via strategic planning and evaluation. We also support for-profits, who are working in the nonprofit sector to start-up and build their enterprise. While I constantly witness the importance of strong talent to our clients, I resisted offering recruitment services for many years. I saw effective talent recruitment as a form of alchemy, requiring special abilities, connections, and a mysterious pool of talent ready to jump at the best job openings. The prices charged by most recruitment firms reinforced this belief; how could any organization charging such high fees not be incredibly specialized and effective? Our clients kept asking for our help in this arena, but I repeatedly declined, politely suggesting a recruiting firm, or, if they couldn't afford one, offering to personally share the open position in my network.

Eventually, a board member I knew well called to ask if we could help him select a search firm for his nonprofit. They needed a new Executive Director and didn't know how to find a recruiting firm that would best fit their specific needs. I obliged by helping them find and vet firms, which ultimately lead to a choice they felt confident in. Within 30 days, we were engaged for a similar project. As the word got out, more and more of these vetting projects followed.

I began to understand the strengths and weaknesses of current approaches to recruiting. From my vantage point, traditional recruiting firms specialized in leveraging their client's networks effectively, finding potential candidates already known to staff, leadership, and board members. They also served as effective project managers, keeping the search process moving and addressing challenges that came up along the way. These firms were adept at matching talent to the requirements of the position, and when necessary, could find talent through their own extensive networks or even via cold calling. However, the latter was not the norm; for the most part, searches were primarily based on the client's own network and candidates responding to job postings.

The weaknesses of the traditional recruitment process also soon became apparent. First, job descriptions were often long and complex. Yes, they provided a vehicle for all search committee members' wants and needs to be included; however, the descriptions were also often overwhelming to candidates, and lacked clarity around essential job functions.

Second, although candidates from the client's networks were well-mined and the pool was further expanded through posting respondents, the cohort of finalists seldom included candidates that were "found" by the recruiting firm. Primarily they were candidates already in the client's network and previously known to them.

Third, key decisions were often "back-ended." In the haste to launch a search, recruiting firms would encourage clients to include a wide array of variables in the job description, rather than taking the time to carefully define the specific criteria for a true best-fit candidate. Often this crucial conversation wouldn't occur until the search committee finally sat down to review applicants. Due to the lack of clarity in the job description, multiple candidates would be disqualified, shrinking the previously robust-seeming list of applicants.

Fourth, despite the strong efforts of the recruitment firms to keep the search on track, it tended to be comparatively slow, resulting in greater pressure on the organization during the transition and often a higher cost of interim staff.

Finally, and most importantly, the professionally-sourced searches I observed cost a great deal of money. There was value produced, but the costs were such that small- and medium-sized nonprofits and corporate firms couldn't afford the services except for their highest positions, if at all. As the result, other key positions were still being filled using internal processes with questionable effectiveness.

Yet, despite seeing the "behind the curtain" view of professional recruitment services, Civitas Strategies continued to vet firms and resist doing the work ourselves. That is, until late 2013, when a long-time client needed to hire for several key positions, resulting from the award of a large government contract. They asked us to recruit for the positions and once again, I declined. They insisted, arguing that Civitas Strategies had a better understanding of their needs and organizational culture than a recruitment firm ever could.

At our client's insistence, I agreed. However, I knew I had to take advantage of the lessons gleamed from watching the traditional process in action. I challenged our team to use our newly-developed understanding of recruitment to design a business model that was equally effective, but would cost half as much and take half the time to implement. If we could come close to meeting this challenge, we would be providing organizations - especially the small- and medium-sized ones most in need – with a significant new tool for recruiting top talent. Though I set the bar high, I never expected we would meet, much less exceed, our goal.

Deconstruction and Reconstruction

The Civitas Strategies team started by dissecting the current recruiting business model, drawing it out using the online system,

Strategyzer, to visually map relevant inputs, processes, and outputs. We also did a deep-dive into the latest recruiting research and practice. We then set about reconstructing the model using three principles of design.

Principle 1: The process is self-executable and modular. Each component was developed so that any organization, for-profit or nonprofit, could implement it without specialized talent or knowledge. We also make it modular; that is, built on several distinct components, so that an organization could choose to implement any one of the component themselves, while opting to contract out others if desired. This prevents organizations from having to make the binary choice of either managing the entire process themselves or hiring a recruiter to complete all facets of the search. This "a la carte" approach allows organizations to obtain external support in the areas they feel it is most needed, while keeping total recruitment costs relatively low.

Principle 2: The crucial step of clearly defining candidate criteria occurs at the beginning of the process. I saw too many scenarios where the rush to get a job open superseded the process of collectively defining what the organization most needed in a candidate. All too often, these decisions were made later in the process - after all the applications were in - forcing the search committee or hiring manager to either settle for a smaller candidate pool or to redo the search with a more specified list of criteria. Instead, we looked for ways to easily force the defining process to occur up front, giving search efforts a laser-like focus towards finding the candidates that best aligned with the organization's needs.

Principle 3: The process primarily utilizes virtual resources. In my observation, the fields with stiff competition for talent (such as bio-tech), make heavy, effective use of headhunting techniques, such as finding people already working in similar positions and reaching out to them by telephone or email. In other words, this is old school *headhunting*: finding proven talent in your field and enticing them to apply for your open position. Headhunting can be a highly effective means for connecting with the best talent, for the simple reason that people performing well in their current roles are often not looking for a new one. However, headhunting is also very expensive, and therefore rarely employed by talent firms supporting nonprofits and smaller businesses because the fees often outweigh the return on the effort. That said, we have discovered through experience that *virtual* headhunting strategies, such as connecting with potential candidates via LinkedIn, are a cost-effective way to reap the benefits of a headhunting practice without the high expense, as the searches are simple and less time-consuming to execute.

The resulting business model, Lean Recruitment, has surpassed our expectations. Our clients' testimonies speak for themselves - they repeatedly report building candidate pools as strong as, and in some cases, stronger than, those developed using traditional recruitment firms. The system also benchmarks at 50% of the total recruitment cost, and takes only 40% of the time needed for traditional recruitment practices. Most importantly, every search using the method thus far has been successful in finding talent as good or better than organizations' past results using traditional recruiting. Also, since the methodology is so cost effective, it has been effectively applied to positions at all levels – including CEO, mid-level managers, and line staff.

For our firm, Civitas Strategies, Lean Recruiting has been catalytic. Since 2014, our recruiting services went from nonexistent to composing 20% of our annual revenue.

The development of this process has also accelerated the creation of other talent management and development services, leading to the launch of Access HR in 2017. Access HR offers specialized recruitment and human resources services to businesses and nonprofit organizations, as well as coaching services for individuals seeking a job change. You can learn more at www.accesshr-systems.com.

In the meantime, we hope you enjoy the book and that it is of great use to you in finding the talent you need for success.

Chapter 1

●　●　●

Lean Recruitment in 3D

L ean Recruitment can be easily executed in three phases (known as the 3Ds, which we will describe below). We found that it can work for almost any position– this process can be used for executives and senior management, but also for mid-level management and line staff. We've also found that using this recruitment approach is effective for both nonprofit organizations with lean budgets (the market we originally developed it for), and for businesses interested in minimizing talent search costs.

The 3D steps of lean recruitment should be executed together, in this order- this is the "secret sauce" of the methodology. Though this is a slim book, there are several steps in the process. To help you along the way, we've included a checklist in Appendix A.

In Phase One, you will **Define**, your organizational leadership needs. The goal is to articulate - clearly and concisely - the capacities, talents, and skills you are looking for in a prospective employee. This is the hardest step of all, since you need to hone in on the most *essential* factors, rather than achieve consensus on a laundry list of items which may intimidate, discourage, or confuse candidates. The effort will require some give and take by everyone on the search team and, accordingly, will take time to complete. But the result will be a faster, more focused, more effective search. By the end of this step, you will have a clear and targeted position announcement that will both articulate what you are looking for in a candidate and showcase the value and virtue of your organization.

The 3 D Process

In Phase Two, you will **Discover** potential candidates. To do so, you will use both active strategies (such as searching your existing network) and more passive approaches (such as posting the job to online). Additionally, we are going to show you how posting to one or two sites and using Internet Bots to leverage the post, will help you reach a wide breadth of candidates. We will also present the most essential steps needed to mine your current network.

In Phase Two, we will also teach you how to virtually headhunt talent; that is proactively search for the talent who best fit your position, based on their current roles. The headhunting process may feel a uncomfortable at first, but there are two significant reasons to include this crucial piece. First, it takes the happenstance out of the equation. Instead of hoping that highly qualified candidates matching your defined criteria happen to see your listing, headhunting allows you to ensure that those candidates see it. Second, it gets your job posting in front of the talent who might not otherwise see it – those who aren't currently looking, but might be open to the possibility should the right posting cross their path.

In Phase Three, you will **Decide** on a candidate. This step includes reviewing, rating, and finally, selecting the perfect candidate. The process begins with a scorecard – a simple tool that will let you and your team impartially rate each candidate (a crucial task supported by substantial research in the human resources field). You will then do short vetting interviews to establish the pool of candidates most worthy of your time during the next component, the formal interview process. Finally, your search team will select your new team member, based on all the information collected.

There is one other point we should address before proceeding. Many times, organizations don't conduct searches because they have a leading internal or external candidate in mind for the position. This is a bad idea. Yes, it may save you some effort, but you also risk shortchanging both your organization and the candidate. Your organization might miss the chance to connect with a more highly-qualified candidate than you imagined existed for the specific role. For the candidate, a quick promotion may undermine their authority with colleagues or cause resentment in other potential candidates who never had the chance to apply, because the job wasn't posted. A simple solution is to implement Lean Recruitment, which mitigates these deficits, with minimal consumption of organizational resources.

Chapter 2

●　●　●

Define

All too often search committees "shoot first and aim later." There is an incredible rush to get the job open and "on the street." When organizations move too quickly, they often take the path of least resistance. The initial rush to release a job has two immediate impacts on developing the job posting (and thereby the whole trajectory of the recruitment effort) - it leads to "recycling" and "laundry lists."

"Recycling" is when the organization quickly grabs text from existing communications for use in the job description. For example, job descriptions typically utilize whatever stock description of the organization is on-hand and easily obtained. Often, the stock descriptor provides basic informational data, such as how big the organization is (e.g. "We serve 6,000 students a year" or "We have a budget of over $23 million"). Stock text typically doesn't cover the information that makes your organization interesting to a prospective candidate, such as why this organization is exciting to work for, potential projects the new candidate could get involved with, or how this position could help build a career.

Concurrently, when organizations rush to post a job, they often create "laundry lists." We've all been there – everyone on the hiring team adds in a few lines about the criteria they personally are looking for or the skills they want the new hire to have. There is no priority given to the most important "must-haves" and no ranking of what skills are a necessity versus a preference. The result is a bewildering mash-up of high-level, all-encompassing ideas and minute details. For example, a laundry list posting might ask for "A minimum of ten years in sales management experience" followed immediately by "Should be able to use Microsoft Office" or "Needs to have a sense of humor." When the position announcement finally goes live, there is little content to inspire candidates and often much to overwhelm them. Such a list can also make it extremely difficult for candidates to accurately assess whether they are a good fit for the position; after a quick glance, many may decide to keep looking.

While moving quickly will get the job position out there, it will also lead to fewer candidates applying for the role. More importantly, it will lead to fewer of the right candidates applying. A cacophony of requirements will overwhelm and confuse candidates, leading to inaction. Of those who do apply, many will lack the qualifications most crucial to effective function in the position, because it is not clear which of the listed qualifications are the priority.

In contrast, Lean Recruitment pushes these decisions to the front end of the process; thereby the posting only contains the most important requirements, providing candidates clarity on the expectations of the role. A good rule of thumb is to state seven requirements, <u>at most</u>. This will require an investment in time and effort upfront for the team to come to a consensus, but the result - greater clarify and focus for both your organization and the candidates, and thus a stronger pool of applicants – is well worth it.

Here is a step-by-step rundown of how the committee goes from deciding to post a position to preparing an announcement that will attract the right talent.

Decision by Committee

Generally, it is good hiring practice to use input from multiple stakeholders. For most jobs, you can use a relatively small selection committee. A typical configuration will include the supervisor for the position; a peer (i.e. somebody at the same level, who will work directly with the hire), a human resource point of contact (if any); and whenever possible/appropriate, a customer or client who will receive services via the hire. (If you work directly with children, it is appropriate to include a parent or guardian). When placing mid-level, senior, or executive positions, we recommend a committee of five to ten members. Depending on the applicability to your organization and the specific position, you could include additional staff, board members, supervisors from other departments, major external partners, or a second customer or client. The inclusion of a representative from an external entity may be uncomfortable for some organizations, as many are not used to including outsiders in their internal decision-making processes. However, this discomfort can be worthwhile for building trust and ensuring the partnerships will continue after the transition. For example, one job search we supported included the nonprofit's funder as a member of the search committee. Though it was initially uncomfortable to talk about internal needs in front of their customer, the honesty did further cement the funder's support for the organization, by providing a better understanding of their needs. It also helped set the new hire up for success, since she was already known to the funder, who agreed she was the best possible choice.

Job Descriptions vs. Job Announcements

Now that you have your hiring committee confirmed, the first task is to develop the scope of the position. As discussed previously, one of the greatest barriers to finding the best talent emerges right at the start of the process in the subtlest of ways; that is the organization begins by developing a job description, rather than a job announcement. Job descriptions are wonderful tools for human resources and management. They help to clarify for everyone what the roles and responsibilities of a specific role are, as well as any other parameters associated with the job. Job descriptions serve their purpose well, but to be clear, that purpose is not to effectively recruit talent.

Accordingly, the first thing we recommend to clients is that they focus on creating a job announcement: a document that clearly describes what skills and capacities are needed to succeed in the given position and gives the audience a clear and enthusiasm-inspiring look at both the role and the organization. Again, this is quite different from a typically traditional job posting, which begins with a brief, uninspired overview of the organization, then launches into a tremendously unachievable laundry list of job requirements. Conventional position descriptions are born out of a desire to make the internal players happy, by ensuring every possible criterion is included. Alternatively, job announcements leave the reader feeling inspired by the opportunity presented, while allowing them to quickly assess whether they possess the most crucial characteristics required.

The Three-Part Job Announcement

Lean Recruitment protocol uses the **Three-Part Job Announcement**. This announcement is more than just a writing exercise – it is a process through which your team will focus efforts by whittling down the requirement list to only the most essential attributes of an ideal candidate. The Three-Part Job Announcement also aims to "sell" the job – that is, making the position and organization as appealing as possible to a potential applicant. This will help grab of the attention of a wide range of candidates – including those not currently seeking a new opportunity.

The sections of the Three-Part Job Announcement are as follows:

* **Section 1: The Where and the Why** – Where is the position located? Why should a candidate consider applying for the job? Why should they consider leaving their current organization for yours?

* **Section 2: The What** – What skills and capabilities are most essential for success in the position and most valuable to your organization? (Remember, this list should include seven criteria at most).
* **Section 3: The How** – How will potential candidates apply for the position? What components need to be included in an application?

Once the hiring committee is ready to author the announcement, we generally recommend sitting down together and working on the announcement section by section. Expect that the announcement will probably go through several iterations; as you discuss sections two and three you may need to go back and edit section one. However, most clients find it most manageable to tackle them one at a time. We also recommend that the committee choose one member to serve as the group facilitator. It may be helpful (and more efficient) to have one member of the team write an initial announcement and then use the committee to refine the text as needed. However, once the initial draft is completed, subsequent versions should be reviewed via a collective meeting (either by video or in-person), as the interplay, discussion, and synergy between contributors ultimately makes the process most effective. Remember - this is not just a writing exercise, but a process for collectively defining success for the search itself.

Before each meeting, the facilitator should plan to send the latest iteration of the announcement and a meeting agenda to the group at least two workdays in advance. During the meeting, the facilitator should begin by reviewing the agenda and any progress made since the last meeting. It is also important to clearly articulate the purpose of the current session, including highlighting any decisions to be made or text to be finalized. At the end of the meeting, the facilitator should clearly articulate next steps, including who is responsible and when the action is due.

As noted earlier, we do not recommend taking on the Lean Recruitment process alone. However, we also recognize that small organizations may, at times, use a search committee of one, due to limited staffing resources. If working alone, we recommend setting aside a minimum of 1-2 hours to develop the first draft of your job announcement. Then wait at least a full day before returning to do subsequent edits.

Please note, as you move through this section, it may be helpful to look at Appendix B which has an actual announcement we have used in the past.

What to Include in Each Section

Section 1: The Where and Why

When writing this section, you will want to think about the following:

* What is exciting and inspiring about your organization?
* What is the nature of the impact you are creating?
* Why is your organization unique or different from other organizations with a similar mission?
* Why would a candidate want to work for you?

Remember what we have learned previously- the best talent probably isn't currently looking for a new position, because they are already experiencing success in their current role. To get the high performers in the field to consider the opportunity you are offering, the description of the position and of your organization needs to motivate them in a direction they may not have been considering.

Draft one to three paragraphs about your organization (the shorter and more succinct, the better), including why an applicant would want to work there. Whenever possible, try to back up superlatives used with names and numbers.

Information you may want to include:

* The primary reasons your organization is a more attractive workplace or has a more innovative mission than others.
* Two to three clients or projects a candidate might find most compelling.
* Growth or impact statistics that will motivate and excite talent.
* Opportunities for promotion or participating in new projects that could help motivate an applicant to apply.

When the search committee is ready to review the results, ask them to do the following:

First, clear their minds of any expectations prior to reading. Second, try to focus on how the announcement would read to someone unfamiliar with organization or to someone with any preconceived notions about the organization's mission or function. Encourage members of the team to take their time. The announcement is your proverbial "first impression" to potential hires, and you may not get a second chance to attract their attention.

Section 2: The What

In this section, the team will front-load the difficult work of establishing focused decision criteria. This is the opposite of the norm, where an organization starts with the lengthy description to narrow the candidates down. They then interview the best and deliberate after. However, in the deliberation process, it is then they realize they didn't need the long list of A, B, C, D, E, and F, but only want A and B and potentially D. Now they have a pool of candidates who may not best fill the most urgent needs of A and B but did somewhat fill their laundry list of A through F. By coming to consensus on candidate priorities up front, you ensure your prospective employees can genuinely "see" themselves clearly in the position and feel confident when applying. This also ensures that you will have the broadest pool of candidates who best meet the most significant needs of the firm. Furthermore, it will help with prioritizing the applicants you want to interview, because anyone not meeting the small but crucial set of identified criteria can be quickly eliminated.

To help with this process, ask the team to answer the following questions regarding their vision for the position (Note: even if the position is long-standing within your organization, it is worth reviewing these questions to check the assumption that the purpose or expectations of the job haven't changed):

* What are the functions of this position in both the short-term and the long-term? For example, is this a position where the ideal hire needs one specific skill-set for the foreseeable future? Or is it a position that you want to grow into something larger over the next 2-3 years? If so, what skills will the new position require?
* Is this a position that will require a lot of on-the-job training? Or do you prefer a candidate who already has the necessary skill set?
* If you are hiring for an existing position, why did the last person leave the role? Is there a way to head off future issues by re-designing or modifying the expectations?
* How crucial is an understanding of your organization, the field, or a specific client-base to achieving success in the role?
* Has the market for talent changed since you last hired for this or a similar position? For example, has a new training program started up, providing more qualified applicants, or has a competitor recently started hiring for similar positions?
* Does the job have to be on-site or can some or all of the role be conducted remotely? (Note: this may be one benefit you would offer to potential talent to help compete with positions offering higher salaries, financial incentives, etc. that your organization cannot afford).

Once the team has answered these questions, you can begin building your list of requirements. Here are a set of questions to guide your thinking:

* What are the three to five criteria the team considers absolute non-negotiables? What characteristics or skills must the ideal candidate have to make them successful in the position or within your organization?
* Beyond this set, what are the next five to seven priorities? Consider education, specific programmatic experience, physical abilities, availability, specific technical or language skills, etc.
* What applicable metrics or thresholds can be added to further clarify your needs? For example, the criterion "Understands public advocacy" is very vague. Instead, your team could decide that the ideal candidate meets the following: "Has led at least two campaigns to change public policy, regardless of their success").

On the team's first attempt to achieve consensus, it may be useful to start by brainstorming all the possibilities, then working together to consolidate, classify, and eliminate until the core set of requirements is agreed upon. Try not to go past the limits established in the bullets above; more than five core requirements and seven additional preferences will start to look like a laundry list. When necessary, remind the team that the process of prioritizing requirements ensures a clear and collective vision for the position, dramatically increasing the likelihood of finding (and keeping) the right person for the role.

It is also important to note in the announcement that your organization is an Equal Opportunity Employer - that is, you do not discriminate based on race, color, religion, sex, sexual orientation, gender identity and expression, national origin, age, marital status, disability, veteran status, genetic information, or any other basis protected by applicable discrimination laws. Your organization may already have an existing statement; if not, we recommend seeking legal counsel on the best wording for your field. You can also go to the Society of Human Resources Managers (www.shrm.org) for guidance.

One more thought, when implementing Lean Recruitment with our clients, we are often asked about salary. More specifically, organizations wonder if they should include the offered salary or salary range in the announcement. When possible, we do recommend including salary information. Here's why: Including salary information helps prospective candidates understand the level of the position and the intensity of the work. Salary information can also serve as an important filter, for both you and a candidate, in determining whether there is a mutual fit. If the hiring team doesn't feel comfortable including salary information, consider highlighting key benefits or other forms of compensation that might help boost a candidate level of interest in the position. Examples might include the possibility of working remotely or at a flexible location, student loan forgiveness, tuition stipends or reimbursement.

Section 3: The How

In this section, you will provide the logistical information candidates need to apply, such as the method of submission, the application deadline, and what to include in the application package. Some thoughts to consider when crafting this section, include:

* Do you require a writing sample?
* Do you want references submitted at this stage or do you prefer to wait until after the interview?

* If now, how many references are necessary?
* Is the deadline for submissions a final date or will you continue to accept applications until the position is filled?
* Can they apply online? In-person? Both?
* If online, does the applicant need to use a specific system or can they just email it?
* Are there any electronic formatting requirements? (e.g., some systems will only accept documents in a PDF format)

It is important that you ask candidates for as much information as possible, so the process continues smoothly into the Decide stage. It is in the best interest of both you and the applicants to avoid pausing the process because you didn't ask for a crucial piece of the application. It is also helpful to ask candidates to send applications to a specially-dedicated email (e.g., recruiting@civstrat.com). This will allow you to avoid filling up your main email inbox, and ensure an application doesn't get missed.

Are we done yet?

Almost. We recommend one more step for quality control: getting feedback from others, outside of the hiring committee. We recommend asking people both internal and external to your organization. You might even consider soliciting feedback from someone who matches your profile for the ideal candidate. For example, if you are hiring for an executive director position, ask an executive director from another, similar organization to comment on the announcement's strengths and weaknesses, and most importantly, whether it would capture their interest. The feedback process is a highly crucial step for ensuring that the announcement crafted speaks to people external to your organization. Furthermore, the perspectives of potential candidates are very important, so don't hesitate to reconvene the search committee to resolve any issues or common weaknesses identified, before going live.

Product Born of Process

Before moving to the next step in Lean Recruitment, it is worth recapping the importance of adhering to the process we have outlined. Lean Recruitment isn't just a way of formatting an announcement; rather, it is a methodology for establishing a clear vision of your ideal candidate and then taking the necessary steps to find that person. It is normal for this process to feel uncomfortable to some members of the search committee at times; by design, not every criterion can end up in the final draft of the announcement. Coming to a consensus may feel difficult, but again, it is worth it to take the time to do so at the outset, rather than trying to backfill the energy later in the process, when the pressure is on to hire.

Finally, though your search committee may become anxious with the time it takes to complete these steps, encourage them to be patient. The decisions you make now will help maximize the effectiveness of the search and save you a tremendous amount of effort and heartache in the last stages of the process or worse, after making a bad hire.

Chapter 3

●　　●　　●

Discover

Once your three-part job announcement is ready to go live, you can begin step three: Discover. In this section, we are going to consider strategies for connecting your announcement with the best possible candidates. In doing so, we will look at both passive and active strategies. **Passive strategies** are the methods you are probably most familiar with, such as posting the announcement on job boards and sharing it in your network via social media. **Active strategies** are not as traditional or typical for small- and medium-sized organizations to use, mainly because they are more expensive, as outlined earlier. Active strategies include networking and headhunting. In this section, we will show you how to use online technology to utilize these strategies quickly and cost-effectively.

Before you jump in to implementing the search, there is a preliminary step we always recommend to clients. Even with the strategies mentioned above, the search for high-caliber candidates can still be very overwhelming. Before you start implementing these steps, take a minute to consider what we refer to as the **Two Wheres**. The Two Wheres are simply the answer to two key questions:

* **Where** are your ideal candidates located geographically?
* **Where** are your idea candidates in their careers?

Again, this step will require some additional effort, but the time invested will pay dividends throughout your entire search, and ultimately in the talent you find for your organization.

Where in the World?

Since the inception of Lean Recruitment, we've learned from experience that the geographic focus of a search should often be much narrower than you might think. This is important because it is a waste of your time and resources to headhunt candidates who meet your criteria, but are unlikely to join your organization. To be clear, geography should be considered when searching for candidates regionally and locally, as well as nationally. For example, commuting patterns in and around a large city such as Washington DC may dictate that you focus your search on candidates currently living or working on the Virginia/Maryland side only, rather than the entire metro area, because these are the commuter suburbs most centrally located to your organization. While you don't want to completely exclude talent from other areas, your efforts will ultimately be more fruitful if you intentionally target areas conducive for commuting to your location.

Yes, there will always be people willing to move or commute to anywhere. But for the majority of candidates, there are limitations to where they are willing to go; factors such as the location of their spouse's job or children's schools and proximity to extended family. As a starting point, consider searching the internet to figure out commuter patterns in your state (for regional or national searches) or the average commute time from various locations (for local searches). State traffic patterns may be more complex than you realize. For example, during one search we did in the southern United States, we found that the target state regularly drew employees from several neighboring states, that were a surprising distance away, but very similar culturally. This information allowed us to expand our search to a larger geographic area than we initially thought was realistic. We have found that online sites such as Google Maps can be useful in mapping which communities are within the average commuting distance of your organization, based on historical traffic patterns and public transportation.

For national and regional searches, it is also important to consider the cost of living in your area relative to the communities from which you may draw talent. For example, Civitas Strategies and Access HR both work with clients located in Florida. Surprisingly, we have found that historically, many Florida residents are originally from the tristate New York area. As a result, potential candidates currently living in the tri-states are often willing to consider positions in Florida, due to the lower cost of living, sunnier climate, and proximity to family and friends who have previously relocated. Thus, when recruiting for positions in urban Florida, we have repeatedly found that cross-posting job announcements in New York, New Jersey, and Connecticut and headhunting candidates from these states to be productive.

Where in Their Careers?

It is equally important to consider the range of experiences your team considers acceptable to ideal for potential candidates. For example, in your job announcement you may have stated a range or threshold to quantify a qualified candidate's skills and experience: "10 years or more of management experience" or "at least three years' experience using Salesforce." However, when reviewing resumes, you may want to consider candidates who fit your threshold but in an unconventional way. That is, who have the appropriate experience, even if it doesn't necessarily fit your threshold in title. For example, when we have supported searches for CEOs, clients always list CEO experience as the top criterion in their job announcement. However, we have also found that COOs from large organizations may have the experience and expertise to serve as the CEO of a smaller company. Conversely, someone with years of CEO experience at a small organization may not be a good fit for a similar position at a much larger firm.

Therefore, it is important to envision the type of position your ideal candidate most likely holds currently. The simplest way is to categorize the position by entry, low, mid, or senior levels. When determining the criteria for each level, consider the following:

* What is the range of experiences they should currently have?
* Do they have direct reports? If so, how many?
* Can they make decisions for the organization? What type and at what level?
* What are their ambitions?
* Are you looking for a candidate who is ready for the next level? Or who needs a few years of experience or skill development before advancing?

Answering these questions before you begin reviewing resumes will serve multiple purposes: First, it will help you quickly eliminate resumes that don't meet your established criteria. Second, it will help focus your search during the headhunting phase, and help you to identify people who fit both your qualifications and your desired salary range.

You may also want to consider the type of organization where your ideal candidate most likely works. What can your organization offer that might be attractive to potential headhunters? You might consider the size of the organization where you plan to look for candidates. For example, small- and medium-sized organizations tend to have a very different culture than large ones. This doesn't mean that if you are a small firm, you should only approach people from other small firms. In some fields, the idea of working for a smaller, more entrepreneurial organization might be very attractive to someone who has previously only worked in large corporations. However, it is something to consider.

You should also consider the focus of the organizations where you plan to look for potential candidates. In some cases, you may want to look at firms similar to your own, because you are interested in a candidate who is familiar with the environment or mission already. In other cases, organizations like yours may be very limited, in which case you need to consider analogous organizations that face similar challenges, or have a similar client base or funders, even though the mission is very different. As further example, we work with nonprofits and varying sizes, and have found a big division between large institutions (such as universities and hospitals) versus smaller, community-based organizations (such as community health centers and after-school programs). In cases such as these, a community health center may be a better employment fit for someone who has worked in a community-based education program than a big city hospital, despite the similar mission.

Spreading the Word

By answering the two "Where" questions, you should now have an even better sense of the potential employee you are looking for. This information will help drive the next step: – using both active and passive strategies to get the word out about the position. Your goal is for the job announcement to reach both the unemployed and currently looking, as well as those who have not been considering a transition…until they hear about the amazing opportunity you have to offer!

Before delving into the details of execution, let's review the three strategies you will need to use. First, you will **post the position online**. Please note - we are going to be very specific on where and how you should post, to keep costs in time and money at a minimum. Second, you are going to **mine your network** (and the networks of colleagues and board members as well!). Many times, the talent you are looking for is someone you already know or are connected to. Third, we're going to look at a cost-effective way to **headhunt online**. Our system will give you all the benefits of a traditional headhunting service, with (again) a minimal investment of time and budget.

Posting the Position

As we discussed earlier, passively posting a job does may get you some applications. However, it is not going to be as large a pool as you could potentially attract; nor is it likely to give you the best possible talent in the pool. (Remember, the highest-quality candidates probably are not actively looking!) At the same time, we don't suggest skipping the step – online postings are a quick and simple way to start.

At this point in the process, the first questions clients ask are:

* "How many sites should I post on?" and
* "How much it going to cost?"

Now, pay attention because this point is very important: We recommend posting your job announcement on **a maximum of three paid job boards or sites**. Here's why: We now live in the era of the **internet robot**. Internet robots are programs that search the Internet for data to put on other sites. We have found that almost every well-known job database, as well as many smaller ones, are fed by Internet robots. Accordingly, if you post on a "feeder site," it will mostly likely get picked up and posted throughout the Internet, within 24 to 48 hours – at no additional cost to your organization!

Therefore, when deciding where to post, we always suggest including at least one large search site; thus, increasing the odds of the announcement getting picked up by the Internet robots. For your other two postings, think about your answers to the two "where" questions and consider the people you described are most likely to frequent. Regional job boards and trade associations relevant to your field are always good options. For example, if you are a nonprofit organization searching for a fundraiser, there are local and regional branches of the Association of Fundraising professionals with their own job boards. Another option is to see if there are affinity groups on LinkedIn or Facebook that may relate to your position, such as the Facebook group for lawyers in your city or a LinkedIn group for working mothers.

Remember, while it may be tempting to add niche sites or trade associations beyond the two we are suggesting, we strongly recommend that stay within the limit. In our experience, the costs of posting in multiple places, both in time and money, can quickly spiral out of control. Furthermore, although posting is an important part of the process, it isn't going to get you the best return on your investment. Accordingly, do post, but please do it sparingly.

Here are some of the bigger job sites we recommend to our clients:

* **Bridgespan** – www.bridgespan.org/jobs - Primarily senior-level nonprofit jobs.
* **CareerBuilder** – www.careerbuilder.com - General job postings across sectors and levels of experience.
* **Dice.com** – www.dice.com - Specifically caters to technology professionals.
* **Idealist.org** – www.idealist.org - Focused on nonprofit opportunities.
* **Indeed** – www.indeed.com - General job postings across sectors and levels of experience.

* **LinkedIn** – www.linkedin.com - Broad site across sectors and levels of experience.
* **Schoolspring** – www.schoolspring.com - Specific site serving the education community.
* **Ladders** – www.theladders.com - Upper level positions primarily in the for-profit sector.

You may also want to consider additional free postings. For example, LinkedIn hosts groups, both open and closed, for college alumni and professionals in a common field. Additionally, some professional associations include free postings on their site. Again, you need to make sure that you are balancing the time it takes to seek out and post on free sites with the possible return it will net you. For example, if you join a regional alumni group of 10,000 members, it may be worth the time to add your posting to their message board. Significantly smaller sites that take effort to seek out, may not be.

Mining your Network

When we vet traditional recruiting firms for clients, we often hear that the highest value they provide is connecting with talent within the networks of the hiring organization's leadership and staff. Despite identifying this value, organizations often skip the crucial step of systematically examining their existing network when self-executing a talent search.

The key to mining your organization's collective network, is to do it systematically and broadly. You want to be strategic about collecting information, to quickly pursue the prospect. For example, a friend or a colleague emailing you a name isn't very helpful, as it will require some of your (valuable) time to figure out what organization they currently work for and their most recent contact information. Whenever possible, get this information upfront! Also, key – you want to share the announcement as broadly as possible. That is, ask all stakeholders in your organization to share the job announcement with their networks, including the executive team, the staff, your board, volunteers, and even external partners.

Most importantly, we have found two specific tools to help make the process of tapping your networks most effective.

First, you want to provide those who will be participating in this process with a simple post that they can share on social media. Social media can be a very effective tool because it sends a much more personalized message to that network than a posting on a job site. Namely, it shows that the person posting the message has some level of investment and excitement about the position. For example, "I enjoy working with ABC, Inc. so much – check out their latest job opening."

Second, it is helpful to provide the people you reach out to with a simple spreadsheet or similar tool. The spreadsheet should provide space to record the name of the person in their network, their current employer and position, and their contact information. Using the same spreadsheet with everyone participating will be helpful when the time comes to aggregate the information. Above all, ask the participant to add both **prospects** and **connectors** to the list. **Prospects** are people in their network they think would make a strong candidate for the job. **Connectors** are people who aren't candidates themselves (for a variety of reasons), but who may be willing to share the position with other prospects.

A little more about connectors: they come in many forms. Sometimes a connector is someone who may or may not be in your field, but who just seems to know everyone. A connector could be someone who, in a role they serve, has access to a pool of prospects, such as the president of a volunteer association related to your field. A connector might be someone in your field and overqualified for the job, but who knows or works with others who might be a better fit. Emphasize with participants that connectors can be just as crucial as prospects to your efforts – you never know who might be the person who connects you to your ideal candidate!

Headhunting

The third strategy in your toolbox is the one that is liable to be most valuable (there is a reason people pay a lot of money for this service!) Headhunting is traditionally very skilled work. However, Lean Recruitment boils it down to a simple process that can be easily executed by your current staff – even if they have never done recruitment work before. The key is to stay focused on the criteria the hiring team has previously established. This seems easy, but amateur headhunters can easily get derailed when they see candidates who might be a good fit for the organization, but not for the specific role – or vice versa. It is also common to start gaining some momentum and then spontaneously decide to expand the scope of the search. It is crucial to stick with the (thoughtful) limitations that have already been set – this is what will keep the process both cost-effective and efficient.

To help the headhunter remain focused, we recommend pulling together a simple one-pager, outlining the criteria you are looking for in a candidate. This includes the requirements and capacities articulated in your job announcement and the Two Wheres. This is for the use of the person searching only, so it is fine (and preferable) to use short sentences or a bulleted list – just enough to keep them on-track and focused on the right type of candidate.

We also find it helpful to set a goal for how many contacts you (or the person doing the headhunting) are aiming to make. Again, when you start headhunting, it is easy to get carried away and find yourself using up much more of your valuable time than you had planned, without the equivalent number of prospects or connectors to show for it. This may vary some depending on the open position, but a good rule of thumb is to aim for identifying 75-100 potential candidates and connectors. This may sound like a lot, but as you begin the process, you will see how rapidly you are able to connect. 75-100 allows for the critical mass needed to generate a significant and high-quality response.

Ideally, you will find a nice balance of potential candidates (people who fit all or most of your search criteria) and connectors (people with a large network that likely includes several potential candidates and who is likely to pass on the position). That last point, "likely to pass on the position," is a crucial one. For example, the CEO of a large organization in your field may know many potential candidates, but they are unlikely to share your posting. A trade association president or the Executive Director of your local chamber of commerce is a much better target.

Finally, before you set out on the hunt, brainstorm a list of where specifically you will look for prospects and connectors. Some thoughts should come easily, such as trade associations in your field. Also consider your two Wheres, and identify the names of companies and organizations where prospects and connectors may currently work. You will come across more as you begin to search, but this will give you some low- hanging fruit to begin targeting.

The Hunt

To organize your search, be sure to create a tracking sheet in Excel to record who you contacted, what their role and organization are, and whether they are a connector or candidate. (You can also download this tool on our website, www.civstrat.com.). Then begin adding names.

Start by adding the easiest targets on your list – connectors whom you already have identified. Then proceed to similar organizations and other institutional targets you have already named. You can also try a broader Internet search - keyword searches for either the type of people you're looking for or the types of organizations where your prospects may already be working. Once you've found some relevant organizations, review the bios on the website to identify potentials for your list. Hopefully you may be able to find their email addresses as well. Another good source for bios and contact emails are webpages covering major conferences and other professional events in your field. They are likely to list presenters with expertise in the area, who might make great connectors. If you can't find their contact information here, or on their organization's webpage, LinkedIn can be a great resource as well.

And speaking of LinkedIn...

Your Recruiting Team - LinkedIn

LinkedIn has truly come into its own over the past few years. Increasingly, it is becoming the new business card – there's an expectation that checking out someone's profile (and having them check out yours) is an expected step in conducting business. In this process, you will use LinkedIn to search for prospects and connectors using that same list of relevant organizations used before. Ask each relevant member of your organization should participate in this step, by searching for their LinkedIn network to see what prospects or connectors they may be connected to. If you aren't familiar with LinkedIn searches, you can "see" the profiles of anyone within one or two network degrees from you. That is, direct connections of your own, as well as their direct connections. This information should help you add more names of prospects and connectors to your spreadsheet.

To see potentials more removed from you, you will need to get a subscription to LinkedIn Recruiter or Recruiter Lite. LinkedIn Recruiter may seem expensive upfront, but you can get a monthly subscription just for the amount of time you plan to use the service. It is also much more cost-effective way than hiring a headhunting firm, and will greatly expand the network of people you are able to connect to. As of the publication date of this book, Recruiter Lite lets you search for, filter, and contact LinkedIn members outside of your immediate network, and includes 30 InMails (i.e. LinkedIn private messages) per month. Recruiter, has a monthly limit of 150 InMails, which are pooled so that any recruiter authorized to access the account can send the allotted number. If you go with Recruiter Lite, you can leverage the limits on the number of emails by identifying candidates and connectors in LinkedIn and then going to the Internet directly to find their contact information. Again, be sure to record all potential prospects and connectors on your spreadsheet as you go, keeping track of how close you are to your target number.

Connecting with Prospects and Connectors

However, you identify your list of prospective candidates and connections, the next step is to make contact. We recommend a simple email format: Start by letting them know about the exciting job opportunity with your organization. Next, let them know that you're reaching out because based on their experience and current position, you think this job will be of strong interest to the people in their network. Politely ask them to share the job with their network and organization. Finally, end with the offer to talk briefly about the position if they have any questions or need further information, and thank them for their time. Of course, you will want to include the link or attachment to the job announcement as well.

We have found this indirect approach to be very effective. Yes, in many cases you are sending this email to people who you think would make an excellent candidate. If they are interested, this email will certainly communicate your interest and hopefully spark theirs. If they are not interested personally, you were still providing a call to action to share it, which will encourage them to pass it on, further into their network. By asking them to share the announcement (rather than directly inviting them to apply), you also avoid putting the receiver into the awkward position of receiving a headhunting communication via an email address they may use in their current role.

Please note, we've included a sample communication in Appendix D.

Diversity as a Hiring Factor

The final section of this book is a selection of Frequently Asked Questions we consistently hear from our clients, with regards to their recruiting efforts. One of the questions we get asked most often concerns diversity; namely, how to factor a commitment to diverse staff into the hiring process. Because we believe strongly in the importance of this commitment in both the for-profit and nonprofit worlds, and because we know many of our clients feel the same, we decided to give this topic its own section, rather than including it as an FAQ.

Ensuring that you were hiring a diverse staff should be a fundamental principle at the core of your talent management system, and specifically regarding recruiting. To be clear, when we talk about diversity, we are applying a very broad definition that includes people of color, all sexual orientations, all gender identities (including transgendered), people with disabilities, and, based on the latest research, people who are neurologically diverse (primarily those on the autism spectrum). There is a clear legal and ethical imperative to ensure every candidate has a fair opportunity to pursue any job. Understanding the legal applications of discrimination law are crucial to your talent management system, but well beyond the scope of this book. That said, beyond the legal requirements, hiring a diverse staff is also a business imperative. Our nation is growing more diverse by the day. This demographic shift necessitates embracing all participants in the labor pool, while also ensuring the demographics of your staff are as reflective as possible of your customers and clients.

When committing to hire a diverse staff, there are several factors, both internal and external to the organization, to consider. Let's begin with internal factors.

As noted earlier, we always recommend that hiring decisions are made by committee. Overall, it is extremely beneficial to involve multiple perspectives and opinions when selecting the ideal candidate. However, the downside of involving multiple parties is that not all search committee members may not be as invested in fully considering the diversity aspect of the hiring process. If this seems to be an overriding issue for your organization – that is to say, most staff members or specific members of the leadership team haven't fully embraced the importance of diversity, consider this a problem to begin tackling as an organization as soon as possible. In our experience, for diversity to be a fully appreciated value of the talent management system, the belief in its importance needs to go beyond one supervisor or manager or even the CEO; rather, the importance needs to be understood at every level. If this is a goal of your organization, there are many great books available on changing company behavior, both generally and specifically regarding diversity, that you may wish to introduce to your team.

The commitment to fostering diversity in recruiting also means that all staff should be ready to look for, and openly confront, behavior that quashes diversity covertly. For example, some companies are using the term "cultural fit" (as in, this candidate doesn't fit our company culture) as an excuse for eliminating diverse candidates without appearing to discriminate. Excuses like this should be confronted head-on, and questioned not only in their veracity but as poor business practice; as previously noted, research shows that organizational diversity is generally a strength.

Finally, consider ways to provide opportunities for existing employees to acquire the skills or capabilities needed to be eligible for future jobs. If you have already done a good job of hiring a diverse staff, this is an effective strategy for ensuring employees stay with your organization, while simultaneously ensuring a strong internal pipeline of talent.

With regards to external factors, clients sometimes note feeling as though the diversity of the applicant pool is out of their control.

However, there are steps you can take to increase the chances of attracting diverse candidates. First, as you decide where to share the job announcement, seek out job boards with associations and organizations that support diverse professionals. Second, commit to continuously expanding your network to include people of all demographics. This will help assure that the next time you conduct a search, you already have a heterogeneous pool of people to pull prospects and connectors from. Third, be ready to talk about diversity with candidates. It may be uncomfortable at first, especially if your organization is relatively homogenous. However, sincere transparency regarding your efforts to improve organizational quality via a more diversified staff is much more likely to elicit interest in your organization than avoiding the topic ever will.

Finally: The Waiting Game

Once you have contacted everyone on your spreadsheet, the waiting game begins. You'll probably begin to receive some applicants on the first day the position is advertised. However, we have found that it usually takes two to three weeks to collect a significant number of applications. It is not unusual to receive applications as late as two months or even longer, after you initially post the position. However, by three to four weeks you should have received most of the applications you can expect. In the next chapter, we will explain the process for efficiently reviewing the resumes you've received.

Chapter 4

●　●　●

Decide

Now that you have a pool of applicants, you must decide what to do with them. One advantage of the Lean Recruitment process is that you are going to end up with many candidates, typically between 50 and 100. The disadvantage, of course, is that this number of applicants can be quite overwhelming. In this chapter, we're going to show you how to start whittling down the pool, using impartial scoring and a simple vetting protocol to identify the best prospects to interview. We will also review the process of interviewing and selecting candidates.

How to Avoid Triage
Many of us have learned to triage applicants in the worst way possible – i.e. leafing through each packet one by one. This approach is pervasive, but inefficient and not nearly as effective as others you can use. First, it requires a high level of talent to execute – someone experienced with hiring who is intimately familiar with the criteria

for the position will need to do it, such as a hiring manager – which your organization may not have. Second, this approach lends itself to cognitive bias, which means that the reader undoubtedly misses a great deal of important information. Different people are naturally drawn to different elements on a resume; it could be anything from the color scheme or font used to a reference to their alma mater. Research is shown our brains naturally focus on the elements most pleasing or memory-inducing, often giving them an outsized impact in the decision-making process, and concurrently creating blind spots to other elements (which may have much greater relevance to the position applied for. Thus, we recommend that instead, application readers use a tool we refer to as **the scorecard**.

The Scorecard

When we set out to develop the Lean Recruitment protocol, we consulted current research on the most effective methods for assessing job candidates. We found that scorecards are highly effective for both triaging and prioritizing a large pool of applicants. The virtue of the scorecard is that it is tied directly to the job announcement, taking the guesswork out of assessing a resume, and forcing the reader to check every criterion listed against the data presented (the resume, the cover letter, work samples, etc.). Also, when done correctly, the scorecard protocol can be implemented by lower-level staff, freeing up managers' time until higher level decision-making needs to be made.

Developing the scorecard is relatively easy, but as you will see, there are points along the way where the search committee will need to make decisions. We recommend using Microsoft Excel, Google Sheets, Apple Numbers, or a similar spreadsheet program. The first column should be the name of the candidate. Every column thereafter will be for a different requirement, capacity, or preference articulated in the announcement.

The next step is to assign a weight to each of the characteristics and preferences. Usually we limit clients to 100 points, which means each candidate will end the process with a score from 0-100. We find this to be the easiest method, since the concept of a "percent grade" is a familiar reference. The allotment of the points should be a consensus decision between members of the search committee, as this will ultimately drive the triage process and will help front-load decision-making about candidates, before you begin to invest time in interviews. When going through this process, clients sometimes get hung up worrying about the relative weight of each variables ("Is education really half a point more important than experience in the field?"). Try not to do this. This process is more art than science, and it is only a triage tool to help eliminate those candidates least qualified based upon your identified criteria. The purpose is to it guide your decision on which candidates move forward in the process, not to make the hiring decision for you. So be diligent, but also know it won't be perfect system – and that's ok.

If you use choose to use gradations, clearly state them up front. For example, instead of having a saying "Experience in the field, up to 5 points," clarify "Experience in the field – less than 3 years equals 2 points; 3 to 5 years equals 3 points and more than five years equals 5 points. Clearly stating these gradations makes the scoring process transparent enough that anyone on staff can help to score the application packages.

As the resumes begin to come in, you can begin to score them using your scorecard. Start by testing two to four applicants against the scorecard and share the results with the hiring manager or search committee. This will give everyone a chance to weigh in on any changes they would like to make before scoring the bulk of the candidates. Once the scorecard is refined, as needed, score the rest of the candidates.

One thought to keep in mind while scoring: if a question comes up, make a note of it on the spreadsheet. For example, maybe you are unsure if a job experience described on the resume fits the type of experience you are looking for. These questions can be answered in the vetting calls if needed (as covered below).

Finding the Cliff

When scoring is complete, look for two interesting features that typically come up during this process. First, the scoring will reveal the trade-offs for each candidate. For example, you may find that the prospective employees with one key identified skill tend to have less experience in the field. The scores will help you see this clearly, and may lead you (or the committee) to decide you are willing to trade off that skill in favor of longevity.

Second, there is typically a scoring "cliff" that becomes no-ticeable when the candidate scores are listed out. That is, the top

10-30% of your pool typically will have scores that are significantly higher than the rest of the pack. The "cliff" is generally very clear - you probably won't have to look too hard to find it. The candidates above the cliff are usually a reasonable cohort for the next step of the process. However, if you decide the number of candidates is too small, consider limiting the cohort to no more than 10-15 candidates.

We typically recommend automatically moving the highest-rated candidates forward. That said, the committee should also be honest about "showstoppers" and "non-starters"; that is, characteristics that you know will preclude hiring the candidate. For example, you may know from their resume that they require a much higher salary than you afford, or a relocation package outside of your means. If you are in doubt or think you could potentially negotiate the issue, include the candidate. But don't move someone forward whom you know could never be selected.

Vetting the Candidates

Now that you have established the cohort of top candidates, you will need to perform one more step before the interview: **vetting calls**. The vetting call, also known as the pre-interview, is a short (20-30 minutes) call used to confirm key pieces of information to help determine whether the candidate should move onto the more intensive (and time-consuming) interview round. There are three parts to an effective vetting call:

1. **Confirm the key requirements**: You will start the call by reviewing with the candidate the basics of the position, including key responsibilities, the job location, salary and benefits (if you are being open about them), and the time commitment required for the position (i.e., full or part-time, occasional travel required, etc.) This may seem obvious, but it never ceases to amaze us how often the most experienced professionals can miss key details. More than once we have had candidates reveal in a vetting interview that they are only interested in remote positions, when the job announcement clearly stated the position was onsite!

2. **Ask lingering questions about the candidate's resume or experience**: As mentioned, questions may have surfaced during the scoring process that you want answered before moving ahead to the formal interview. We recommend keeping questions as precise as possible, to limit the scope of the call. For example, instead of asking "Tell me more about your experience at ABC company," ask "When you were at ABC company, how engaged were you with strategic planning?" Also, be sure to ask them how they found out about the job. This will give you some insight around the effectiveness of your recruitment efforts. It is also useful data for refining your strategy, when using Lean Recruitment in the future. You should also inquire directly about a candidate's salary requirements – this crucial step may save you from proceeding further with a candidate whose expectations are way beyond your budget.

3. **Answer the candidate's questions** – Ask if they have any questions for you. When in doubt, let them know you will get back to them with an answer to ensure accuracy - hiring is not a situation to guess at answers. They will probably ask about next steps in the process. Many times, though the next step may seem clear, as you deliberate the process will increase in time, so consider a vague response along the lines of: "We will start our deliberations soon and will let you know about next steps either way."

Generally, we find that about 25% of the candidates in your original cohort will be eliminated during the vetting process, either because you decide they are not a good fit, or because the candidate realizes the position will not work for them. This is a good thing, as the reduction in the size will make the interview phase all that more efficient.

Almost there!

Once vetting is complete, you are now very close to conducting the formal interviews. First, you will need to select the candidates to move forward to the final phase. Four to five candidates is ideal; we suggest no more than ten at the most. At this stage in the game, you should be able to identify the candidates that most closely match the ideal you outlined at the beginning of the process. It is a waste of both your time and the candidates to interview people you know have very little shot of receiving an offer. If the top four to five don't pan out, you can always go back and select a few more from the cohort to interview. Conversely, once you have invested the time in prepping and conducting the interview, you can't get it back.

For each candidate in the interview pool, create a profile for the search committee. The profile is essentially an executive summary of the candidate. and should include an overview of their qualifications, as well as any specific information from the process thus far distinguishes them from others. Also plan to include any unanswered questions you or the committee has for the candidate.

The Interview

You're finally there - the interview! Interview protocol can and should be differentiated to your organization and its particular needs. Generally, we recommend a process that includes a final pool of four to five candidates and one round of interviews, with a second round only if needed. (For example, if the committee can't make a final decision without a specific piece of additional information). The interviews should be conducted by your entire search committee; at minimum, the hiring manager or position supervisor, a peer, and if appropriate, a client or consumer of your goods and services should participate. (Please note, the selection of this individual will need to be made very carefully, since it requires giving a person external to your organization a transparent view of a highly sensitive, internal process. However, clients can also provide extremely valuable feedback on candidates and are often able to give a perspective very different from that of organization staff, so it may be worth considering). Our preference is for group interviews, (i.e. one candidate and the committee) since they are typically more time-effective. If by necessity, the interview will be conducted remotely (as opposed to in person), connect via an Internet video service. This way everyone can observe both the candidate's reactions and body language, in addition to hearing their responses.

So now the big question: What do you ask the candidate?

We strongly recommend avoiding the tried-and-true questions focused information you already have or that is easily attainable; questions such as how many years they were at a position, or what skills and strengths they will bring to the job. Instead, we recommend focusing on what are commonly referred to as **behavioral questions**. Behavioral questions are interview questions designed to give the interviewer powerful insight into the candidate's values and mindset, by asking them to describe scenarios that demonstrate their demeanor and attitudes towards work and exemplify how they typically react to various situations and challenges. Asking behavior questions enables the committee to gain a sense of how the interviewee will approach problems, respond to colleagues and clients, and whether the candidate is able to think on their feet. Examples of typical behavioral questions include:

* Have you ever gone above and beyond your job responsibilities? If so, how? Why?
* Tell us about a time you worked effectively under a deadline, including what strategies you used to achieve success.
* Describe a difficult situation with a colleague/supervisor. How did you handle it?
* Give an example of a time you set a goal, and how you went about achieving it?

See Appendix C for more sources on behavioral interview questions, including the ones we recommend frequently to our clients.

It is very important to develop your questions thoughtfully, and subsequently to and assign specific questions to each interviewer ahead of time. Whenever we conduct group interviews, we always include the question assignments in the Interview Protocol, a document which clearly lays out the interview agenda (including timing), and a script for the committee of exactly what should be asked and when. This will greatly reduce the risk of an inappropriate question being asked, and ensure that all key topics are covered. The Interview Protocol is also an effective tool for keeping the committee on-task and adhering to a tight timeline. As the head of the interview team, you may also want to identify key words or phrases that you're looking for in each answer. This will help the team members to clearly understand the responses considered most valuable.

During the interview, it is helpful to assign a host or facilitator, responsible for guiding the session and keeping track of time. This person should start the interview by introducing all members of the team, as well as their position within the organization, to the candidate. Try keep the interview to an hour or an hour and a half maximum; beyond that the returns rapidly diminish due to mental exhaustion. Always reserve at least 25% of the allotted time for the candidate's questions to you. This is more than a courtesy – the types of questions asked may give you even greater insight into their suitability for your organization.

The Decision

Once the interviews are complete, the search committee can hone in on which candidate to offer the position. Make sure everyone on the committee is clear as to who has the ultimate authority in this decision. For example, does the CEO or hiring manager have the final decision, or can the majority vote of the group prevail? This is important to state upfront, in case the majority of the team and organizational leadership are not in agreement. By making this hierarchy clear from the get-go, you are preventing disappointment and loss of morale later. If there is ultimately one person making the decision, it doesn't preclude the engagement of the group to comment or provide their opinion. The point is to ensure that the mechanism for final decision-making is transparent.

You may want to start with an initial vote from the group, to get a sense of where the majority thinking lies. Typically, in this initial vote, we'll find that the group has gravitated to a subset of one to three candidates. The committee can then review each one of these candidates in further detail, with each member commenting on the individual's strengths and weaknesses. Additional votes can help to clarify whether group opinion has shifted as the result of the debate. However, at some point the committee will need to put an end to the discussion. It is very rare for everyone on the search committee to agree on one candidate. More typically, the decision will lack the consensus of one or more members, even after extensive debate.

Another scenario we have witnessed is the team determining that none of the candidates are the right fit for the position. If that's the case, we strongly recommend interviewing a new group of candidates, rather than settling for the "lesser of the evils" in the current candidate pool. To select a candidate that does not have the general support of the deciding body, is to set that individual up for failure, in a position or organization for which they are not a good fit.

Once a decision has been made, don't forget to notify everyone who applied for the position. This simple courtesy is normally expected, and deservedly so, out of respect for the time and effort the individual put into applying for the job. Your reply does not need to be lengthy or explanatory; a simply thank you for their time, and a statement that the search committee has gone in a different direction will suffice. At times, you may have candidate who has not been selected for interview, but who reaches out to you before you have made the decision. In this situation, we recommend that you send a brief response, letting him or her know that you are still deliberating. This is an honest reflection of your status, and, as mentioned above, you never know when you may need to reengage other people in the original pool.

Chapter 5

●　●　●

Now What?

You've completed the process of Lean Recruiting – but you aren't quite done. As we mentioned at the start, the competition for talent is fierce and the resources your organization can devote to recruiting are likely to stay level, at best. Ensuring you are as effective and efficient when implementing this process is key. Therefore, we recommend that in between Lean Recruitment searches, your organization continuously uses the following three talent-related strategies, expanded on below:

1. **Always Be Looking.**
2. **Track Effectiveness.**
3. **Share Knowledge.**

Always be Looking

Simply put, we recommend that you should "always be looking" for talent. Yes, you may not be ready to hire someone at that moment, and the people you find may not be ready to be hired right now either. However, identifying and tracking prospects you know would be a good fit for your organization or specific positions within your organization can accelerate the search process in the future.

To "always be looking" does not necessarily mean engaging a tremendous amount of time on speculative candidates. Instead, it's the process of paying attention to the people in your network for who seem particularly adept at skills valuable to the work your organization does. It might mean keeping an eye out on LinkedIn for the up and comers in your field and region, observing who is making job changes, getting promoted, or adding new skills. If a particularly interesting prospect arises, you may want to reach out and connect with them. If you choose to reach out, we recommend being transparent upfront about your intentions. Let them know that you don't currently have an open position, but that you find them interesting and would appreciate staying in touch. You can also use the opportunity to delve further into their skills, interests, and ambitions. Even if you end up deciding that the candidate is not a good fit for your firm, you have built another connection in your field that may be valuable in the future.

Also important - Ensure that the process of "always be looking" doesn't just rest with you, but with those who report to you as well. Securing the best talent for your organization benefits everyone, and therefore should be considered a shared burden.

Tracking Effectiveness

Depending on the size of your organization and frequency of hiring needs, we recommend you undertake some simple measures, to both gauge the effectiveness of your efforts and inform future searches. These measures are simple, and do not take up a lot of your time, but will net you valuable information. In fact, these are the same measures we used internally at Civitas Strategies to inform the development of Lean Recruitment, and now use at Access HR to continually refine the process to best suit the needs of our clients.

There are two measures we primarily rely upon and recommend to clients:

1. **Cost Per Hire**
2. **Source Effectiveness**
3. **Pool Pipeline**

Let's take a closer look at each one.

Cost per hire is a simple ratio demonstrating the quantity of resources consumed when hiring a given position. It should consider all the costs of the hiring process, from the moment the process began to the finalist accepting the position. These costs might include the following:

* Time invested internally for a search.
* Posting fees on job boards.
* Any travel, meal, or lodging costs for the interview process.
* Costs for consultants, if used.

Tally the total cost, then divide this number by the total number of hires for the process. Consider the following example:

Company X conducted a search for a new project manager. When the search concluded, they listed their costs as the following:

* Salary and benefits for 3 days, supporting the recruiting efforts the firm's Executive Assistant, the position supervisor, and a line worker who served as the search committee - $5,550.
* Posting the position on two job sites - $250
* Parking for the five candidates who were interviewed - $100

The total cost of Company X's search was $5,900. Since they only hired one person, the cost per hire was **1:5900** (or, one hire cost $5,900). If they had been able to fill two jobs from the search, their cost per hire would reduce to **2:5900** or **1:2950** – one hire cost half the price at $2,950.00

The second measure we use is **Source Effectiveness.** Source effectiveness is simply the number of interviewees derived from a given source. For example, if you have an interview pool of 10, you may find that:

* 2 candidates heard about the job via a LinkedIn posting,
* 6 candidates received emails as part of your headhunting efforts,
* 2 candidates were referred by an existing employee, and
* 0 candidates heard about the job via a posting on your local association job board.

By doing this quick analysis, you can quickly see the importance of using headhunting in future searches. Conversely, if you find that the trend for zero interviewees from the association job board continues, you may want to stop posting there and try another resource instead. (Remember, even if the posting is free, your time if not -why invest in an endeavor with no return?) To be clear, we suggest tracking "interviewees" over "everyone who applied" since, in the age of the Internet, there are people who use their own bots to apply for many jobs, as quickly as possible (whether they are qualified or not). By focusing on the selected interviewees, you are rating your sources to determine which one(s) produce the best results, rather than the one where the most Internet robots found the posting.

The final measure is **pool pipeline**. Pool pipeline is simply how many people applied for the position versus how many were interviewed. This data will provide you with information on two points: First, how good of a job your search efforts did at attracting strong candidates. Second, the strength of the final interview pool. For example, if you conduct two simultaneous searches, you may find you have 100 applicants for the first, with seven candidates interviewed, and 75 applicants for the second, with two candidates interviewed. This data indicates that the first search attracted a higher percentage of quality applicants (7%) than the second (closer to 3%). It may be worth your time to examine if there were any significant differences in how the two searches were conducted.

For those of you who hire new candidates infrequently (say once a year or less), or who only hire one candidate at a time, these data points may not be extremely relevant. However, for those of you who hire for more than one position a year, the resulting data may help you understand how to invest your recruiting time and dollars more effectively. You might also consider tracking the diversity of candidates following each search. It is important for the health of your organization to reach out beyond your existing connections and ensure you are seeking out the best talent, offering different or new perspectives on your field. Accordingly, tracking the number of candidates who are people of color, disabled, or meet other sub-group criteria, will help you determine how to best ensure diversity in your search.

Share Knowledge

We want to leave you at the same place we started- there is an on-going talent war and nonprofits and small and medium businesses are at a keen disadvantage. As your organization benefits from Lean Recruitment, others can too – so please spread the word! We welcome any feedback you have on further refining or improving this process, so that we can continue to develop the best recruiting tool possible. Reach out to us on our website at **www.civstrat.com** or **www.accesshrsystems.com.**

Frequently Asked Questions

Below are some of the questions we hear often from clients regarding the recruitment process, as well as Gary's responses.

Q: I don't want to share the salary for our position in the job announcement. I fear it will provide too much information for existing employees and risk throwing off our pay structure. It is essential that I include it?

A: Ideally you want to mitigate risk by including salary and benefit information - and by risk, I mean risk to you and prospective candidates. Salary information helps job seekers develop a clearer sense of the fit between the job with their personal background and needs. Which in turn means fewer false leads for you. However, there are times you won't want to share salary information. If this is the case, consider sharing benefits that could inform candidates. For example, "We have a generous healthcare plan and contribute up to 5% of salary per year towards retirement." Not sharing any compensation information should be a last resort only.

Q: Should I give preference to an internal candidate?

A: The best course for you and your organization is to keep an open mind to all talent – internal and external. Studies have shown repeatedly that there are advantages to hiring internally, such as familiarity with the organization and processes. However, one can argue that these benefits are equally matched by the benefits of hiring externally, such as gaining a fresh perspective and new network connections.

Accordingly, we recommend creating a job announcement that is inviting to internal and external candidates alike. For example, if you have a propriety database you use, instead of saying experience with XYZ database (which would openly favor the internal candidate) consider something that covers the category of systems like "experience with relational databases." Additionally, we typically recommend interviewing all interested internal candidates if possible, as a courtesy to your existing employees.

Q: What do you think of practical exercises or portfolios as part of an interview process?

A: I think both can have value, but do take the time necessary to execute well. In either case, I would ensure your selection committee articulates very clear criteria on what you are looking for and how the product will be scored. I recommend using a score- card similar to the one we use to assess applicants. By proactively setting clear criteria and values, the search committee members can then judge the practical exercise or portfolio fairly, efficiently, and effectively.

Q: Do you recommend using a consultant for recruiting purposes?

A: We created Lean Recruiting in hopes that small- and medium-sized businesses and nonprofits, could use the system to level the talent playing field, without the cost of consultant services. Accordingly, this process should be entirely self-executable. However, there are two cases where you may want to consider engaging a consultant. First, if your staff entirely lacks the time to execute all facets of the system we outlined. In this situation, you may want to consider using temporary administrative staff or a similar resource to execute Lean Recruiting, as an alternative to engaging a more expensive recruiting firm. Second, you may want stronger technical expertise for specific components of the process. For example, Access HR may be engaged to help construct the job announcement and to headhunt candidates, while the client self-implements all other steps. This "modular" approach is one of the key design elements of Lean Recruiting. By outlining a set of distinct tasks, organizations can engage outside help carefully and judiciously, to best minimize costs.

Q: Is okay to ask candidates to complete an application in addition to sending a resume?

A: Yes. We often recommend using an application. Applications give you the option of obtaining additional information, not present on a resume or other materials sent by a candidate.

Q: I'm not sure what the salary should be for a position new to my organization.

How do you recommend figuring this out?

A: If you are not sure what the salary (or salary range) for a position should be, you have two choices. The first is to have a professional salary survey done.

Firms like Civitas Strategies and Access HR are often engaged for short-term research projects like this. However, if a professional survey is out of your budget, it is possible to conduct one yourself. It will take a bit of effort on your part, but can be done using the following three steps:

1. Identify a cohort of organizations similar to your own. You are looking for firms or organizations that are as like yours as possible; consider mission, size, geography, type of staff hired (highly experienced vs mid-level experience vs inexperienced), etc. Competitor companies can be particularly useful for this exercise.

2. Do your homework. See what you can find out about the salary ranges each organization in the cohort offers. One resource to try is the website Glassdoor (www.glassdoor.com). You can also try searching the internet for old job postings for positions similar to the one you are trying to fill – you may be able to gleam salary information there. Don't forget to check the organization's personal webpage, which may include job postings or other

salary and benefit information as well, particularly if you are looking at large-sized organizations.

3. Analyze the information you find to come up with a suitable range for your position. If you can't find postings for the exact position you are filling, look for positions with similar requirements, in terms of education, years in the field, and required skills. This should give you a sense of what is reasonable, even if the responsibilities of the two positions are different. If you can find applicable postings from a variety of companies, it may be helpful to look at a posting from a lower-paying company, a mid-range company, and a high-paying company, to best understand the scope of the range of salaries in your region or state. That said, we always tell clients that it is critical to be realistic about what you can afford. It is usually not in your organization's best interest to overtax the budget hiring a top performer in your field, when less-experienced, but more affordable candidates could do the job well. Alternatively, consider what benefits you could offer top talent in lieu of a higher salary, such as a flexible work schedule or the opportunity to work remotely.

Q: Should I confirm with candidates when applications are received?

A: Yes, it is a good practice to create a stock email saying you have received the applicant's materials. Keep it short and to the point. For example: "Thank you for applying for the XXXX Specialist position with ABC, Inc. We are undertaking a thorough, but potentially lengthy process. We will get back to you if you are selected or not, so please expect a communication later in the process."

Q: What should I do if we are still determining who to hire and a candidate we have already ruled out contacts me for a status check?

A: It is important to treat inquiries from viable candidates and those you have eliminated in the same way. Simply thank them for their effort and let them know you are still deliberating. For example, "Thank you for your inquiry concerning the XXXX Specialist Position. We received a great number of applicants and are still deliberating. We will notify all applicants when the process is complete."

Appendix A

●　　●　　●

Lean Recruitment Checklist

STEP 1 – DEFINE

• • •

Get very clear about the job you're trying to place

Three-Part Job Announcement

Part One – Organization Description: *Draft one to two paragraphs about your organization, focusing on why an applicant would want to work there. Be sure to include:*

* At least one reason your organization is more attractive than others.
* Two to three compelling clients or projects that you work with.
* The statistics of your growth and impact that will motivate and excite talent.

Part Two - Position Description and Requirements: *Set the key criteria that are **most essential** success in the position you are filling.*

1. Start by writing down <u>all</u> the possible skills, abilities, and qualifications that your ideal candidate will have. Be sure to use clear and specific metrics and thresholds whenever possible. (e.g. "Has led at least two campaigns to change public policy in the last five years, regardless of their success").
2. Consolidate your original list by highlighting <u>three to five</u> core requirements.
3. Identify the next <u>five to seven</u> 'lesser' (i.e. preferred but optional) requirements.

Part Three - The Fine Print: *Include all details on how to apply for the position.*

* Where candidates should submit their application. (Note: consider a dedicated email for the position, such as associateconsultant@civstrat.com).
* What documents the applicant should include (e.g. resume, cover letter, writing sample, letters of recommendation, etc.)
* Statement about equal opportunity employment

Scorecard Creation
Using your finalized Position Description and Requirements, create your Scorecard in a spreadsheet or similar tool.

* Assign weighted scores for each characteristic based on what you believe is most crucial for success. Limit yourself

to 100 points and distribute them among the characteristics so that each candidate ends up with a score between 0 and 100.

* Consider the use of gradations and be sure to clearly state them up front

* For example: "Experience in public housing, Up to 5 points"
    * Fewer than three years [2 points];
    * More than three but fewer than five years [3 points];
    * More than five years [5 points]).

• • •

STEP 2 – DISCOVER

• • •

Strategies for distributing and selling the job

The Two Wheres

* Where will the ideal candidate be located geographically?
  * National?
  * Local?
  * Anywhere at all (remote position)?
  * Similar cultures, where cost of living differentials is the similar?
* Where will the ideal candidate be in their career?
  * Level of decision-making?
  * Types of organizations (for-profit or non-profit; large or small; similar or related)?
  * Credentials?
  * Years of experience?
  * Specific skills?

Distribution Channels

* Share with your network (e.g. ask people in your personal network, relevant staff members, and clients to share the announcement with their network) – may want to provide

participants with a simple announcement for use on social media and a spreadsheet to track names and contact information of potential prospects and connectors

* Post on **one** 'Feeder' Job Board (e.g. Idealist.org, Bridgespan, Indeed)
* Post on one to two additional sites (consider small but targeted niche sites, such as your professional association's job board)
* Headhunt potential prospects and connectors via LinkedIn and the Internet (e.g. Guidestar)

STEP 3 – DECIDE

• • •

Hone in on your final choice

* Score Applicants
* Determine your top cohort using your applicant 'cliff' (limit your cohort to no more than 10-15 candidates)
* Hold vetting calls to ensure that candidates are interested in the job as is (e.g. hours, salary range or other requirements, such as having to be on-site)
* Develop Interview Protocol, including interview questions and assignments
* Interviews
* Set decision expectations (e.g. Who will decide - the group or one person) and execute

***REMEMBER:** Always be looking: *You may not be hiring immediately, but establishing connections with interesting individuals in your field will help inform future recruitment efforts. Also, track your effectiveness per Chapter 5 so you have data to inform your next process.*

● ● ●

Sample Three-Part Job Announcement

Title: Consulting Associate
Location: Virtual Office (company based in Lynnfield, MA)
Position: Part-time, as needed project support
Compensation: Hourly, commensurate with experience

Civitas Strategies, is a management consultancy that contributes to the betterment of children and families' lives by helping public-serving organizations grow, via strategy design and the crafting of sustainable business models. Our clients do the truly noble work, in the trenches, with children and families. We enable a broad base of clients to reach more families and children, by refining their strategy and sustaining their impact. Our commitment to community is not only in our client service, but also our pro bono projects, carbon neutral operations, and corporate giving program, which totals over 15% of our annual net profit.

The Position:

The Consulting Associate will be responsible for providing as needed, self-managed support on a project-basis.

Tasks include:

* Conducting research to understand market trends and issues.
* Collecting and analyzing data.
* Proofreading and editing reports, proposals, emails, web content, and
* other written communications.
* Developing client-ready documents including memoranda, presentations,
* and brief reports.

Core Qualifications

* Bachelor's degree required.
* Evidenced passion for social impact, education, or a related field.
* Ability to meet deadlines, manage a flexible schedule, and work independently and collaboratively.
* Strong verbal and written communication skills with a demonstrated ability to write clearly.

To Apply

To apply, please send a resume, cover letter, and two writing samples to recruiting@civstrat.com. Applications will be reviewed as they are received.

Civitas Strategies, LLC is an Equal Employment Opportunity (EEO) employer and does not discriminate in any employer/employee relations based on race, color, religion, sex, sexual orientation, gender identity and expression, national origin, age, marital status, disability, veteran status, genetic information or any other basis protected by applicable discrimination laws.

Appendix C

• • •

Interview Questions

These sites offer vetted interview questions for your selection process:

* The Society for Human Resource Management: *Has an extensive list, but it is behind the membership firewall. However, the list is excellent and worth a membership alone (SHRM offers other value for organizations with little or no internal HR capacity).*
  https://www.shrm.org/resourcesandtools/tools-and-samples/interview-questions/pages/default.aspx
* Glassdoor: *Offers the top 50 interview questions. Some will be very familiar or even seem cliché, but are effective nonetheless.*
  https://www.glassdoor.com/blog/common-interview-questions/
* The Muse: *Offers an excellent list of common behavioral questions that will apply to most jobs and sectors.*

https://www.themuse.com/advice/30-behavioral-interview-questions-you-should-be-ready-to-answer

* RecruitLoop: *Offers 75 more behavioral questions.* http://recruitloop.com/blog/behavioural-interview-questions/

Here's a sampling of the questions we at Access HR often suggest to our clients:

1. *Tell me about a time that you had to give negative feedback to a colleague. How did you prepare for the conversation? How did the conversation go?*
2. *How do you approach learning about a new organization or project?*
3. *How have you used data to make a point or sway a decision at work in your favor?*
4. *Describe a time you had to handle a difficult client or customer? What did you do to calm them down? How did you address their concern?*
5. *What excites you the most about working for our organization?*
6. *How would you describe your management style? Give us an example of how it has played out in the workplace.*
7. *Tell me about a time that you had to say "no" to a customer or client. How did you approach the conversation? What was the result?*
8. *What is your single greatest professional achievement? Why?*
9. *What is the next skill or capacity you want to develop professionally?*
10. *When working in a group, what role do you play?*

Appendix D

• • •

Sample Headhunting Email (For use with both prospects and connectors)

July 27, 2017

Dear Candidate,

I am emailing on behalf of **XXX**, an organization committed to providing high-quality program evaluation services for nonprofit organizations, about a new position that is now available. XXX has recently experienced exponential growth and is current looking for an **Evaluation Manager**.

I'm hoping you can share this opportunity with your network to support XXX's important mission.

The Evaluation Manager will lead the development of internal data collection and analysis systems for all the organization's programs. Additionally, they will help develop and oversee all independent evaluations.

Attached is the full position announcement. All interested applicants should send a resume and cover letter to jobs@ accesshrsystems.com.

Thank you so much and please don't hesitate to reach out to me if you would like further information or have any questions.

Sincerely,
Gary Romano
Access HR

About the Authors

Gary Romano founded Civitas Strategies in 2010 to provide high-quality, cost-effective management consulting to for- and nonprofits working to serve the common good. The firm quickly took off, and has recently led to the launch of the spin-off company Access HR which provides cost-effective talent management and recruitment services, as well as coaching for individuals looking for new jobs.

With more than 20 years of management and consulting experience, Gary has extensive expertise helping organizations move from vision to implementation. Gary holds a Masters in Urban Affairs from Virginia Tech and a Bachelors of the Arts from Stony Brook University

Alison LaRocca is the Engagement Manager for Civitas Strategies, where she plays a key role in leading a variety of client projects. She specializes in helping clients to increase their social impact through strategy design and implementation. Alison also serves as a principal consultant with Access HR, helping clients to design affordable and sustainable talent management solutions.

Prior to joining Civitas Strategies, Alison taught at the award-winning Community Day Charter Public School (CDCPS) located in Lawrence, MA. Alison holds a Masters of Education from Merrimack College and a Bachelor of Arts in History from Williams College.